So the Vicar's Leaving . . .

The good interregnum guide

Mike Alexander
and
Jeremy Martineau

With illustrations by
'Ron'

CANTERBURY PRESS
Norwich

in association with
ACORA Publishing

First published in 1998
Reprinted 1999 by ACORA Publishing
Arthur Rank Centre, Stoneleigh Park
Warwickshire CV8 2LZ

Revised edition published in 2002
in association with Acora Publishing
by the Canterbury Press Norwich
(a publishing imprint of Hymns Ancient &
Modern Limited, a registered charity)
St Mary's Works, St Mary's Plain
Norwich, Norfolk NR3 3BH

www.scm-canterburypress.co.uk

British Library Cataloguing in Publication data

A catalogue record for this book is available
from the British Library

ISBN 1-85311-505-3

Typeset by Regent Typesetting, London
Printed by Creative Print and Design, Wales

Contents

Acknowledgements

The authors are grateful to diocesan secretaries, bishops and others for providing appropriate material from their dioceses. We are indebted to the Revd Ian Hardaker for many of the ideas in the section on interviewing the prospective vicar. We also record our thanks to churchwardens, area/rural deans, clergy, diocesan secretaries, archdeacons and bishops who read an early draft of the report and offered comments. Finally we acknowledge our indebtedness to 'Ron', the *Church Times* cartoonist, for his humorous illustrations.

Note on the second edition

For this second edition, we have incorporated a few improvements and made alterations in the light of changed circumstances.

Foreword

The prospect that there will be a few months without a vicar creates mixed feelings in many parishes. Tears, whether of sorrow or relief, are often replaced by anxiety, even blind panic, about all the things there are to do. The problem sometimes is finding out what needs to be done and who should do it.

That's where this book is so valuable. It is full of common sense, humour and clarity – a reliable guide at what can be an uncertain time. And it shows us how spirtually creative the interregnum can be. I am delighted to welcome this new edition and hope that it will continue to be widely used.

† Graham James
Bishop of Norwich
April 2002

Related titles available from ACORA Publishing

**Rural Ministry: A parish work book for lay ministry
in the country church**
  Leslie J. Francis, Keith Littler, Jeremy Martineau
A practical training guide to aspects of worship, pastoral care
and church management
0-95168-716-6   128pp   £10.00

Rural Visitors: A parish work book on relating to visitors and tourists
  Leslie J. Francis, Jeremy Martineau
How to make your church an effective sign of the kingdom, even when
it's empty.
0-95407-660-5   128pp   £10.00

The Servant Church: Organising rural community care
  Elfrida Savigear
A guide to good practice in church-based community care.
0-95186-713-1   32pp   £3.50

ACORA titles are available from the Canterbury Press
Find out more about these titles on our website:
www.scm.canterburypress.co.uk

Introduction

In this book, we explore a range of issues related to what the Church still refers to as an interregnum ('between reigns'), although some prefer the term vacancy. Both terms are misleading as lay people take on more responsibility in today's church and collaborative or shared approaches to ministry become more common. Throughout this book we shall attempt to avoid both these terms and talk about the time when the parish is without a vicar. We shall also use the term 'vicar' to include 'rector' and in preference to the more formal 'incumbent'.

When the vicar leaves, no matter how well the parish is organised there will be a need for clear planning. The main focus will be on the period when there is no vicar – how to cope and how to flourish. However, this period does not fit neatly in a box; it is a transitional period in a parish's life. It is necessary to place it within a longer timespan, to examine the time leading up to the vicar leaving and the arrival of the new vicar and the 'settling in' period.

In this period between vicars there is a need to handle several matters:

- how to keep parish life going
- discussions over a replacement for the outgoing vicar
- taking on board a whole range of items dealt with by the vicar – from the minor administrative tasks to major pastoral and planning issues
- the presence of a curate, licensed readers, non-stipendiary ministers and retired clergy.

Problems may emerge:

- there may be a leadership vacuum and a jostling for power
- the decision making process may be unclear

• there may be confusion over the roles of churchwardens, the PCC and the area/rural dean.

We have written this book primarily for churchwardens who are at the sharp end. We hope that what we offer will help them face up to a challenging task with confidence. However, others – area/rural deans, PCC members, outgoing and incoming vicars as well as curates, licensed readers, non-stipendiary ministers and other church leaders – will also find useful information here.

The Reverend Herbert Lemmon realised it was time to retire

Chapter 1

Not just another Sunday morning

It's another Sunday morning, much like any other as you set off for church. Most of the regulars are there although a few familiar faces are absent. The service goes well and then at the end of the service the vicar makes an announcement:

'I have been invited to become the vicar of a new parish and I shall be leaving in about two to three months. Now is not the time for farewells, but I want to say how much I have valued your friendship and support during my ministry here.'

The situation will differ, the words of the announcement will vary, but somewhere each Sunday this type of scene will take place.

Imagine this is your church. If you are a regular member of the congregation, but not deeply involved in church life, how do you feel?

Is it a case of vicars come, vicars go but life goes on, or was this one somewhat different – a bit special or a dead loss? Are you thinking "Thank goodness, we won't have to suffer those long-winded sermons for much longer" or is it 'We'll never get anyone who is as good with young people'? Are you already wondering how long the parish will be without a vicar? You may have heard it said that an interregnum is one of the best things that can happen to a parish and wonder whether that can be true. All kinds of thoughts will be going through your mind, some of which you might want to talk to others about, others that you would rather keep to yourself.

If you are a member of the Parochial Church Council (PCC), how do you feel?

You may share some of the thoughts that any regular church member feels. However, there is an added dimension. You have worked with the vicar on the decision-making body of the church. Are you wondering how the PCC is going to function without the vicar or are you already beginning to see it as an opportunity to get things done? You might also be wondering what to say when the PCC is asked about the type of vicar wanted next.

If you are a churchwarden, you might have known for a few hours, a few days or a few weeks that the vicar is about to leave. How do you feel now that it is public knowledge?

Are you thinking how others must be feeling and wanting to talk to as many people as possible, or are you thinking of the work you have to take on during an interregnum and wanting people to recognise this and offer words of encouragement?

If you are the vicar, you will have known for some time that you are on the move.

In most cases, there will have been delicate, often secret discussions over the new parish. You will have had to work through some difficult decisions. Is this move right for me (and, if you have a family, is it right for them)? Do I really want to leave this parish and these people? Is this really God's will for me? How do you feel now that you have announced that you are leaving?

For some of you the interregnum may be a present reality. For others it is about to begin. For others it may be some time in the future.

Every parish and parishioner will experience something of the pain, joy, challenge, loss and gain that comes with an interregnum. We have highlighted the most common ending to a vicar's ministry in a parish, namely moving to another parish. There are other endings – death, retirement, leaving the ministry – that will bring out different emotions and feelings.

In one sense nothing will be the same again as the parish moves on to a new phase of ministry. However, God is there, ahead of us, inviting us into the future – in faith.

Not just another Sunday morning

Chapter 2

It's never too early

Thinking Ahead

It is never too early to prepare for that time when the parish will be without a vicar. While this book suggests many practical tasks, it assumes that these activities will be undergirded with prayer without which all will be in vain.

A small group of lay people, authorised by the PCC, could start by drawing up a list of the major areas of church life and the activities carried out under each of these headings.

Listed below are a few examples:

In worship:
- Who arranges the rotas for flower arrangers, preachers, service takers, sidespersons, lesson readers, intercession leaders, the offertory procession and who chooses the hymns?

In pastoral care:
- Who is responsible for visiting newcomers to the church, those who are ill at home or in hospital, the bereaved and parents bringing their children for baptism?

In relating to the local schools:
- Are there schools where the vicar or other members of the congregation take assemblies, visit staff or provide help in religious education classes and who does it? Is the vicar or any other member of the congregation a school governor?

Through this investigation, the group will begin to discover who is responsible for what. They will also clearly identify what the vicar does.

They might also go on to consider how decisions are made in each of these areas of work. Is it left to those who carry out the work on behalf of the church? Do they seek advice from the vicar and where does the PCC fit into all this? Through asking these questions, they will build up a picture of the church's work and the way it is organised.

Addressing the Issues

Before facing the period without a vicar, address some of the issues raised. If the vicar is responsible for a significant number of the activities, the PCC might consider allocating some of the tasks to others. At the very least, someone needs to know how the vicar carries out the activities for which only he/she has responsibility. This will ensure that you overlook nothing when the vicar goes and someone knows how each activity is organised.

If the vicar is responsible for the care and support of most of the leaders of the various activities, it may now be the time to involve members of the PCC in taking on some of this work. At the very least, you need to know the type of care and support that the vicar offers.

The collecting of this information can never start too soon. It may need doing bit by bit. It will also need updating from time to time. It may lead to more lay involvement. It will undoubtedly prepare the parish for that time when the vicar leaves.

Once the vicar decides to move on, the PCC needs to consider which of these jobs are essential and, for those that are, who is to take responsibility. It may be difficult to find volunteers for some of the jobs. Some people will need to consider giving up a job for which they now have responsibility to oversee a more important job that is currently the vicar's responsibility. Some jobs may need to be left undone – the PCC secretary should make a note of these jobs and the reason for leaving them. This will be useful information for the new vicar as it may show that some jobs are unnecessary whereas others that have been on the 'back burner' now need to receive attention.

When the vicar leaves, the patron becomes a key player in the appointment of the new vicar. To help the patron take his/her responsibility for the parish seriously, invite him/her to join in its worship and meet members of the PCC. In this way he/she will be much better informed about the parish and its needs. This will result in better co-operation when the time comes for the patron to exercise the prime responsibility of finding a new vicar.

The parish lost no opportunity to advertise

Chapter 3

Accentuate the positive

A Positive Approach

Once it is known that the vicar is leaving, anxiety can arise. The parish may feel like a ship without a captain, drifting aimlessly on the open sea. An important part of facing up to this challenge is to set clear objectives for the first six months. These objectives should link to the overall aim of the church. In each area of the church's life, clear objectives will give purpose and confidence.

In a parish where the vicar and lay people have learned to work together, the period without a vicar should build upon those achievements and prepare for the work with the next vicar. It is a time for steady growth and development.

Situations differ, however. A parish that has suffered from a lack of enthusiasm or commitment in its outgoing vicar may wish to try new things or develop the neglected aspects of the church's ministry. If the PCC, in collaboration with the churchwardens, fully supports these developments, real growth might begin, which most new vicars will appreciate. At the same time, the PCC needs to ensure that any developments are appropriate to the parish. It is radical change, going 'against the grain' of the parish's life, that can cause instability and alarm.

On the other hand, the parish may have had a 'ten new ideas before breakfast' vicar. This may be the point to begin to assess things. Are there some good ideas that never 'took off' and need further thought? Are there schemes that are not working and need to end? Are there people working on one of the previous vicar's ideas of which the PCC is unaware? A systematic review will help to bring things together before the arrival of the new vicar.

The Approach to Change

It is sometimes thought that 'those in authority' at a diocesan level want nothing to change during this period. This is not always an accurate perception and a conversation with the area/rural dean will clarify this.

It is not always easy to have a clear, consistent view with regard to change. Some change is inevitable over a period of six-nine months, the average length of time from one vicar leaving to the next arriving. People may resign from a church post and a replacement is essential. A group may come to a natural end and disband. New initiatives may seem entirely appropriate. The role of the PCC is to monitor such changes and give approval where this is necessary. Some changes have such profound implications for the life of the parish that it may be unwise to introduce them when the parish is without the mediating role of the vicar.

The churchwardens may need to consult with the area/rural dean over whether to introduce a particular change or await the arrival of the new vicar. However, ultimately it is the PCC's decision as to what happens during this period. It needs to adopt a sensitive approach to issues of change whilst guarding against stagnation.

Before the Vicar Moves

The outgoing vicar will have a significant amount of information in his/her filing system or memory. Primarily there are three things to discover:

- What the vicar does in the different areas of the church's ministry
- Who is responsible for areas of work that are not the vicar's responsibility
- The unusual, occasional items that only the vicar knows about.

Several meetings with the vicar may be necessary to pass on all the vital information.

Some clergy organise their administration well; others detest any form of paperwork and may need careful sympathetic treatment in the process of retrieving essential information. Whatever the outgoing vicar's approach, the churchwardens should arrange to meet with the vicar to plan the handover. Ideally this should happen at least two months before the vicar leaves. It is helpful to organise the information into categories:

- Information that can be shredded or thrown away
- Information to keep for the churchwardens and PCC to use
- Historical records that may need to be deposited with the county archivist
- Information to leave in confidence for the next vicar.

Many clergy now use computers. If the computer is parish property, someone with a knowledge of computers should meet with the vicar to discover the software in use and ensure that he/she leaves the instruction books. You may need to print on paper (known as 'hard copy' in computer language) any parish information stored on computer. If the computer is the property of the vicar, it is absolutely imperative that all information relevant to the life and work of the parish is on 'hard copy'. In addition, someone should copy the information stored on computer to 'floppy disks or zip drives' and keep them in a safe place.

Hopefully the vicar will offer information in a spirit of openness. He/she needs to understand what the parish will need when he/she has gone. A diary of regular activities over the past year may prove helpful in making sure that things are not overlooked when there is no vicar. Some clergy, sometimes for good reasons, want to plan the next few months for the parish. This might be tempting, but it is probably better for this to be done by the churchwardens, leaving the outgoing vicar to tidy up loose ends and prepare for moving.

The Churchwardens were not caught entirely unprepared

Communication

Good communication is essential to ensure the smooth running of parish life, particularly when the vicar, one of the main channels of communication, is no longer there. The churchwardens should begin to draw up a list of key people, including addresses, telephone and fax numbers and E-mail addresses. This list is likely to include the patron, bishop, archdeacon, area/rural dean, diocesan staff, PCC officers, church members with specific responsibilities, clergy and licensed readers on the service rota, organist, verger, undertakers, architect, local builders and others.

The churchwardens and the PCC members take on a key role in this period. The churchwardens and the PCC officers should meet regularly. PCC members need to take responsibility for different aspects of the church's life during the time when there is no vicar and to ensure that jobs are done. Good communication with the regular members of the church is essential, encouraging their involvement in the life of the church. They also deserve to be kept informed, without breaching confidentiality, on progress in the search for a new vicar.

The weekly notice-sheet is an important part of the communication with church members. The parish magazine provides an opportunity to show that the church's worship and life are continuing and that it is worth becoming a part of it. At all costs, avoid putting over the message that "without a vicar, there is no church". It also offers the opportunity to communicate information on practical arrangements while the parish is without a vicar. This might include a list giving the names, addresses and telephone numbers of those responsible for different areas of the church's work.

The church notice board is another important link with the community. It often covers a dual purpose, advertising worship and social events organised by the church and giving the point of contact with the church, usually the vicar's address and telephone number. When there is no vicar, it is essential to continue using it to highlight what is happening in the church and to give the names and telephone numbers of those now handling enquiries for baptisms, weddings, etc.

When There is More than One Parish

Where parishes are linked together in a larger benefice, the departure of the vicar can reveal holes in what should be a system of trust and co-operation between neighbouring churches. On the other hand, it can bring parishes closer together. It may be possible to share some duties rather than for each set of churchwardens to carry on without reference to the others. Now is the time for churchwardens to plan together. A meeting of all churchwardens chaired by the area/rural dean is the first step. Avoid subsequent confusion by preparing a list of who is responsible for what in the wider benefice.

Some of the issues relating to linked parishes may need sensitive handling:

- If the present number of services is reduced, carefully consider the effect upon each church. It may help to arrange an occasional joint service in a different church each time.
- The sharing of costs may be more complicated when there is no vicar. If lay people are working across parish boundaries and reasonably claiming expenses, there is a need for clear procedures for paying and allocating such expenses. There may be other costs, such as the redecoration of the vicarage and the refreshments after the service of institution, that parishes need to share.
- The venue for the institution service may be a contentious issue. In a situation where only one church in the benefice has the seating capacity for such a service, the decision is usually straightforward. Where there is more than one suitable venue, the choice may be more difficult. If it is decided to use a different venue each time, this needs the agreement of the PCCs and the decision clearly understood so that there is no argument next time around.

Chapter 4

Saying goodbye

How to Say Goodbye

Some clergy prefer to leave quietly, taking their normal Sunday services before the removal vans appear. Others prefer an opportunity to celebrate the relationships formed and the work achieved together in a final act of worship and/or social evening. Farewells are a time of mixed emotions, for those leaving and those who remain.

Saying goodbye

The churchwardens and PCC have to consider on behalf of the regular members of the church how to mark this significant moment in the parish's life. This requires careful thought as to the vicar's needs and the parish's needs. It is important for this to be a joint decision.

Saying goodbye is important. There is a need to mark the end of the vicar's ministry in some way, even where the leaving event is to be 'low-key'. This will help to avoid subsequent feelings of guilt based upon a sense of unfinished business.

A joint decision on whom to invite to the final event is also helpful. There may be special friends or colleagues of the outgoing vicar who would like to attend. The vicar may appreciate it if someone arranges for these invitations to go out.

The churchwardens and the PCC have to decide how to organise the contributions towards a leaving gift. It is normal practice to keep this secret from the outgoing vicar (even though everyone, including the vicar, knows that it is happening!) and that can make it difficult to publicise. One way is to distribute a sheet with the magazine, giving details of the collection, who to make cheques payable to and where to send contributions.

Moving house incurs extra expenditure. Consider whether to give a small personal gift with the bulk of the contributions as a cheque. Someone can make sensitive enquiries as what to buy if the vicar would appreciate a gift using part of the money given.

The Leaving Service

The leaving service can be one of at least two options:

• A special service, normally arranged for an evening in the week before or after the vicar's final Sunday services
• Included in the services on the final Sunday.

With their farewell collection, the Lemmons took a cruise

Factors to be considered include:

- What would suit the majority of church members?
- Are there representatives of the wider community who might wish to be there?
- Is it being combined with a social gathering?

Once the vicar and the churchwardens/PCC have agreed on the best arrangements, the details of the service can be considered.

A leaving service may include the following:

- Giving thanks to God for all the achievements during the vicar's ministry here
- Looking back at the role of the church in this community over the years
- Asking forgiveness for schemes that have failed and people who are feeling hurt

- Looking forward to the challenges that are ahead
- Praying for the parish(es) to which the vicar is moving or the retirement about to begin
- Praying for those who will choose the new vicar
- Praying for those who exercise a continuing ministry in the parish
- Praying for those who will have a key responsibility during the time when there is no vicar
- Saying goodbye
- Reminding those present that the parish is the local expression of a worldwide timeless church.

There is no set liturgy for such an occasion but it is helpful to have a focus. It may make sense to find a theme that expresses the way in which the vicar and church members have attempted to work together. Alternatively, the focus may be on the way the parish sees its role at the moment. This theme can pull together all the aspects mentioned above.

Final Social Gathering

Depending on the tradition of the church, this event may be as significant as the leaving service. What kind of occasion is appropriate, the 'normal' social event or a different approach, as this is not a 'normal' event in the social calendar? In deciding, be aware of the needs of the outgoing vicar and family and the needs of church members.

Some ideas to consider:

- A 'This was your life whilst here' presentation with various people offering their stories – amusing, embarrassing, serious and profound
- An audio-visual presentation of the major events and changes that took place during the outgoing vicar's ministry.

Whatever is done, make sure that it is appropriate. Avoid hurting anyone. Do not attempt anything too ambitious or beyond the scope of what has been done before. Imagine what the event would be like if the outgoing vicar were organising it for someone else.

Review of Ministry

If the PCC has worked in this way before, it may be appropriate at the final PCC meeting before the vicar moves for some kind of review of ministry during the vicar's time in the parish. This might take around 30–40 minutes or be extended to a full meeting. The information gleaned will not only be a of help in the 'leaving process', it may prove to be a valuable contribution in assessing the current state of the parish and its future needs. Someone other than the vicar should facilitate this part of the meeting. Ask the person in the diocese responsible for lay training to recommend someone with adult education skills to get the most out of this sharing together. In such sharing people need to be clear about what they are being asked to do and how to share the information. They should offer only what feels appropriate.

Listed below are a few possible ways of doing this:

- *The PCC considers the changes that have taken place during the outgoing vicar's ministry*
  This can happen through small groups focusing on different aspects of the church's life, e.g. worship, teaching, pastoral care, evangelism, church buildings, social activities, youth work, etc. As far as possible, a factual rather than judgmental approach is more appropriate at this stage. Record each of the group's points on a flip chart or overhead projector. An optional second part is possible. This involves considering the changes that have taken place over the same timespan in the wider church, the local community and the world.

- *An assessment of priorities*
  This involves individual work and sharing together. The outgoing vicar receives a sheet of paper with four statements on it:
  In my working with the PCC
  the main priorities have been . . .
  difficulties have been over . . .
  the most successful things have been . . .
  the least successful things have been . . .
  Each member of the PCC has a sheet with the phrase 'In my working with the PCC' being replaced by 'As a member of the PCC working with the vicar'. The sharing at the end requires honesty with sensitivity.

- *An opportunity to express 'thanks' and 'regrets'*
  Each member of the PCC receives a sheet of paper with the outgoing
  vicar's name on the top and two statements (I thank you for . . . /
  I regret that you have not . . .). The outgoing vicar's paper has the name
  of the parish at the top and two statements (I thank you for . . . / I regret
  that you have not . . .). A simple way of sharing is to go quickly around
  asking each member of the PCC to offer one thing that they regret. The
  vicar then offers his/her list. A similar sharing of things they wish to
  give thanks for then follows.

Parish Consultation

This may also be a good time to bring church members together to look
at achievements and to plan for the future. You may decide to invite all
members of the church to a consultation on a Saturday (say 10am to
4pm) or a Sunday after the morning service through to tea. If carried out
early enough, the parish profile can take account of the information
gathered from the consultation and help in deciding on the type of vicar
the parish needs. As with a review of ministry, an experienced adult
educator will help to get the best out of such a day.

The day might cover the following areas:

- Strengths and weaknesses of the parish
- What the outgoing vicar did
- What lay people do now
- Areas where lay people might become more involved
- What the new vicar might offer
- Difficult and sensitive issues that a potential vicar needs to know.

In addition, there may be time to look at what the church was like
three–five years ago, what it is like today and what it hopes to be in
three–five years' time. Alternatively, concentrate on setting goals for the
next six-twelve months.

Chapter 5

Working with others

Duties of Churchwardens

Churchwardens have a key role to play at this significant time in a parish's life. Working closely with the area/rural dean they are responsible for two basic items:

- Arranging cover for church services
- Ensuring that the PCC meets regularly.

Once the vicar has moved, the churchwardens may feel that the whole burden of responsibility has fallen on their shoulders; for others the authority given can turn their heads. It is important to remember the two main areas for which the churchwardens have responsibility working alongside the area/rural dean. All the other decisions are the responsibility of the PCC. Churchwardens will need to be aware of the important items and bring them to the PCC's attention. They should not take on everything themselves. However, there will be items that churchwardens will have to deal with on behalf of the PCC. This is often an ideal time to involve other lay people and to delegate tasks wherever possible.

The churchwardens are responsible for ensuring that the PCC meets. There is normally a vice-chair who may or may not be one of the churchwardens. The churchwardens should meet with the vice-chair, PCC secretary and, where it functions as an agenda planning group, the PCC standing committee. It is vital that the PCC retains its decision-making role and does not 'pass the buck' to the churchwardens.

Working with the Area/rural Dean

Churchwardens need to develop a good working relationship with the area/rural dean, who has a crucial role in supporting and encouraging them. There is also a duty to ensure that the parish follows proper procedures. Getting the right balance between the two is an art.

Along with the churchwardens the area/rural dean has responsibility for ensuring that worship and parish life continues once the vicar has left. The area/rural dean is the first person to ask about the legal and diocesan procedures following the vicar's announcement that he/she is moving.

The area/rural dean sometimes meets with the outgoing vicar. This meeting provides an opportunity to share information that will help the

The arrival of the Rural Dean

area/rural dean regarding potential problems and opportunities for development. The area/rural dean can also offer advice as to what information the outgoing vicar should leave for his/her successor and for the churchwardens and PCC.

Around two months before the vicar leaves, the area/rural dean will usually arrange a meeting with the churchwardens. This will allow the churchwardens to share any concerns they have, to talk through their approach to the months ahead and to decide how best to organise service cover. If this does not happen, the churchwardens should ask for such a meeting.

If your outgoing vicar is also the area/rural dean, the churchwardens may need to ask the archdeacon about alternative arrangements and for advice in the absence of a area/rural dean.

Working with Each Other

Churchwardens should work closely together throughout this important phase of the parish's life. We have considered the work that is the responsibility of the churchwardens and the area/rural dean. In practice, the area/rural dean is the point of reference for advice and support, while the responsibility for carrying out the work rests with the churchwardens and the PCC. Each churchwarden will have different abilities and interests. Decide whether to share tasks or tackle them together. Consider bringing in other people to help. Agree on who to approach and be clear about what you want them to do. If they agree to do it, give them clear directions, advice, support and training where necessary. The PCC should endorse this devolved responsibility.

Having done all this, there will be tasks left that someone has to do. Decide between you whether it is better to do these together or to share them between you. Whatever you decide, it is vital that you offer each other genuine support and encouragement.

In a multi-parish benefice, you need to work out what to share across the whole benefice and what to work on at your own parish level. We raised some of the issues that may occur in the section 'When there is more than one parish'. If you are in this situation, it may be advisable to re-read that section.

Working with the PCC

According to canon law, it is the duty of the vicar and the PCC to consult together on matters of general concern and importance to the parish. In addition it is the function of the PCC to co-operate with the vicar in promoting the whole mission of the church – pastoral, evangelistic, social and ecumenical.

It is equally important that, when there is no vicar, the churchwardens work in a co-operative way with the PCC. Regular meetings of the churchwardens with the vice-chair and secretary of the PCC are essential. Churchwardens need to keep the PCC informed of important matters, allow its members to discuss items of concern and make decisions on matters of policy.

Working with Other Members of the Congregation

The churchwardens and the PCC will find that involving regular church members in the full range of activities during the time when you are without a vicar lightens the load. Do this in a way that allows people to use their gifts, gives them responsibility and offers them support and encouragement. Be clear about each person's responsibilities.

In chapters 1 and 2 we set out ways of discovering the work that the PCC needs to cover. The gaps will become clear once there is a list of all the key tasks and the people who have responsibility for them. As we suggested earlier, some of these may have to be set aside. It is not possible to do everything when you are without a vicar. The PCC may authorise a small group of people, who are skilled at discerning gifts in others, to consider who to approach to take responsibility for the key tasks that are not yet covered.

Once the key tasks fall within the brief of members of the congregation, it may be that you can draw others in to carry out some of the smaller tasks. This may go wider than the regular church attenders. Some people on the fringe of church life may be willing to take on a simple piece of work, e.g. delivering a few parish magazines in their street. It may even draw them into a commitment to the church.

Obviously the range and frequency of the tasks and the number of people drawn in will depend upon the size and strength of the church. However, the more people become involved, the greater their commitment will be. Hopefully this will carry over into the period when the new vicar is in place.

Working with Readers and Other Authorised Lay Ministers

The role of licensed readers varies from parish to parish. Some involve themselves in all aspects of parish life and are part of the ministry team. Others may have to limit the number of services they can take or the times they can preach. If there is a licensed reader or licensed readers in the parish, an early meeting with the churchwardens and the area/rural dean will help to clarify their role in this period when the parish is without a vicar.

If one of the churchwardens is also a licensed reader, the other church-warden needs to be sensitive to the pressures on his or her colleague. It may be that the work of churchwarden takes priority and the licensed reader/churchwarden takes fewer services or preaches less. There may be other licensed readers who can help out with worship so that the licensed reader who is also a churchwarden can carry out the important duties required.

There is a danger that licensed readers who have preached regularly at the main communion service lose that opportunity when there is no vicar. In planning service cover the churchwardens need to bear this in mind and, from time to time, have the parish licensed reader preaching with the visiting minister presiding at the communion service.

Licensed readers in a parish where there is no vicar may be asked to cover too many non-communion services. As well as deciding whether to reduce the number of services, you may need to consider fixing a limit on how many services a licensed reader should lead and how often he or she should preach in a month.

There may also be other authorised lay people in the parish. The church-wardens and PCC need to ensure that they:

- are properly authorised
- know their responsibilities
- do not take on extra work without proper authority.

Working with Curates and Other Clergy

Issues of authority and accountability may arise where there is a curate or non-stipendiary minister. The curate or non-stipendiary minister is not in charge but he/she is the one wearing the dog collar. Many people, inside and outside the church, will turn to the ordained person for advice and help.

This may be particularly difficult for the curate at whatever stage in the curacy this occurs. The curate will find that a number of key things have changed. As well as having all kinds of expectations placed upon him/her, the curate has lost a colleague and, in some cases, a close friend and role model. He/she no longer has a training incumbent. The person responsible for the training of curates at a diocesan level may appoint a senior colleague to help the curate with her or his training needs. If no alternative arrangements are made, the churchwardens may need to ask, probably through the area/rural dean, what help is available. The churchwardens should work closely with the curate and the senior col-league who will supervise the curate's training to ensure that together they offer appropriate training, support and advice.

The impact upon the non-stipendiary minister will depend upon the role he/she has in the parish. We recognise that the title can mislead. Some see themselves primarily as ministers in secular employment with limited involvement in their local church. Others take a fuller part in the church activities. The churchwardens need to ensure that he/she is able to contribute in a way that is appropriate to their circumstances.

Sensitivity to the feelings of a curate or non-stipendiary minister at this time is crucial. Churchwardens need to meet regularly with the curate or non-stipendiary minister to clarify who is responsible for what and to ensure the smooth running of parish life.

There may also be retired clergy or clergy from other denominations who have close involvement with the parish. In this case, consider their position carefully so that they are neither overburdened nor underemployed.

During the interregnum, retired clergy were
always willing to take services

Chapter 6

Worship and pastoral care

Vital Areas of Church Life

In a book of this size and scope, we cannot consider every aspect of church life. The parish's size, traditions, approach to mission and ministry and its priorities will determine its involvement in different aspects of church life. However, there are two areas of church life for which the vicar usually has a major responsibility.

These are:

- Worship, including what are known as the occasional offices (baptisms, weddings and funerals)
- Pastoral care.

In any church, no matter how small, these are issues that need handling well during the time when there is no vicar.

Arranging Worship Cover

It is the area/rural dean and churchwardens' responsibility to plan service cover. At an initial meeting, consider the best way to arrange this. It is helpful to examine the number and range of services provided at present to see whether there are to be any changes; take any changes to the PCC for their approval.

Draw up a list of clergy – retired clergy, diocesan advisers and non-stipendiary ministers – who might help out. Contact each of them to check out whether they are able to help, how many services a month they are willing to take and their preferences regarding the type and time of services. The area/rural dean may also be willing to lead an occasional service and the bishop and the archdeacon may appreciate an invitation.

Draw up a list of licensed readers, bearing in mind the type of non-communion services there are, e.g. evensong, 'family' service, 'praise' service.

In some dioceses there is a system in place for arranging licensed reader cover. In some deaneries the area/rural dean's secretary makes the initial contact with clergy and licensed readers. In some parishes a curate, non-stipendiary minister or licensed reader in the parish will agree to co-ordinate this. Whoever is responsible for arranging cover should list the services over a three-month period taking into account any seasonal variations. Having checked out the general availability of clergy and licensed readers and drawn up a shortlist, telephone and discover what they can do in this first period. Do not leave all those with limited availability until last as there may be few dates left to offer them.

Draw up a chart giving full details of the dates, times, readings, form of service (i.e. Common Worship, BCP, etc.) and the names of people officiating. Circulate this to the area/rural dean, churchwardens, the clergy and licensed readers who are officiating, organist and choirmaster, and display a copy in the vestry and at the back of the church. Halfway through the three-month cycle, it is advisable to start on the next three-month's cover so that the person responsible can finalise it and sent it out four weeks beforehand.

Circulate notes on the liturgy used to visiting clergy and licensed readers. It may help also to enclose a full order of service highlighting the parts for which the visiting clergy or licensed reader has responsibility.

Sunday Worship

The church's most important activity is its worship of God. Church officials are sometimes spiritually malnourished because they have practical duties in arranging worship. For some it becomes a performance rather than an uplifting occasion. Good preparation will ensure that everything runs smoothly and that there is an opportunity for all to worship God.

One of the churchwardens should be in church 25–30 minutes before the service begins. Begin your preparation with a time of quiet prayer. When the visiting minister or licensed reader arrives, show him or her the layout of the church – vicar's stall, lectern, pulpit – and talk about the usual practice and how far the congregation can cope with alternative ways of doing things. If the visiting minister or licensed reader is to give out the notices, read the banns or pray for the sick and departed by name, please ensure that this is made clear and the information is legible.

The visitor may have questions about what happens at various points in the service. Keep a copy of the notes for visiting clergy and licensed readers in the vestry so they can refer to them quickly.

Even with the best-laid plans, there may be an occasion when the visiting minister or licensed reader fails to arrive for a service. If this happens, it is the churchwardens' responsibility to ensure that some form of worship takes place. It makes sense to keep the following in a convenient place for such an eventuality:

- a *Common Worship* Book
- a *Book of Common Prayer*
- *Patterns for Worship*
- the lectionary
- a general book of prayers
- a book of intercessions
- books of readings on biblical texts or religious themes.

You will find a list of resources at the end of this book. Churchwardens are authorised to lead worship in an emergency. If it is an Common Worship communion service, those leading worship can follow the normal service up to the Peace, with a reading instead of the sermon. With morning or evening prayer, the full service is possible. Only an ordained priest can give absolution following confession but the person leading the worship can use an alternative form of words.

If the visiting minister or licensed reader has not arrived five minutes before the service, start organising the books you will need to lead worship. Decide who will lead the worship and begin to sort out the readings, prayers and an alternative to the sermon. If the visiting minister or licensed reader has still not turned up by the time the service is due to begin, make an announcement to the congregation. Explain the situation and let people know what will happen if he/she does not arrive in the next 5–10 minutes. In churches where members of the congregation are willing to take part, ask for volunteers to read lessons, prayers and the reading instead of the sermon. Familiarise yourself with the service, make a note of the hymns and where they come in the service, and write down the names of those reading lessons or leading the prayers. Do not rush but, once you are ready, begin the service. If the visiting minister or licensed reader arrives during the service, keep the service going until there is an appropriate point to hand over.

Baptisms and Wedding Enquiries

Make sure that the system for handling baptism and wedding enquiries is clearly understood. If the vicar has previously handled this or the vicarage has been the place for such enquiries, then the PCC may need to decide who can take on this task and how best to handle enquiries. In setting up a procedure for such enquiries, the needs of those coming to book a baptism or a wedding should be balanced against the demands on the person willing to deal with such enquiries. Publicising a particular time and place for such enquiries will probably be adequate.

The people who now receive the phone calls to the vicarage need to know the procedure to deal with enquiries or pass them on to the person now responsible for this aspect of the church's work. Churchwardens may be able to deal with the difficult issues that may arise. If not, the area/rural dean is the person to contact for guidance.

There is normally a form for booking baptisms. Those responsible for arranging the baptism and the preparation of the parents and godparents need to have these forms and be fully briefed about how to proceed.

If there is an agreed policy on baptism, the PCC needs to decide how to

Not every person can lead worship

implement it when there is no vicar. If the vicar has been responsible for the preparation of parents and godparents, set up alternative arrangements, after advice from the area/rural dean. Most churches, except where large numbers make this difficult, include baptisms in their normal Sunday morning service. Discuss any change to this practice with the area/rural dean.

Booking a wedding is a more complicated procedure. It will be helpful for the person taking on this role, with possibly one of the churchwardens, to have a session with the outgoing vicar going through the procedures. There is a form to fill in, but there are often extra items (choice of hymns, choir, bells, etc.) that do not appear on standard forms. The minister taking the service will require a copy of this form. The person willing to write up the wedding registers and the certificate needs to know how to do this. In addition, a return of marriage entries is completed at the end of each quarter. This requires the signature of the area/rural dean before being sent to the local registrar. If the person responsible for booking weddings has any questions on what to do, the area/rural dean will offer advice.

There will also be couples who are to marry in another church who wish to have their banns read. There are strict rules governing when to read banns in church. They will also require a certificate for which there is a fixed fee. The person responsible for booking weddings and the reading of banns needs to understand the system well.

A practical issue regarding preparing couples for marriage may arise. Unless there is an organised preparation session for those about to marry, the vicar is likely to have prepared the couple. It is probably better for the person who is to take the wedding also to handle the preparation. However, this needs to be made clear when booking clergy for weddings.

If there is no agreed parish policy on the remarriage of divorced persons, it is usual to follow the outgoing vicar's approach, if this is in accordance with diocesan policy. Once again, a conversation with the area/rural dean will help to clarify things.

Baptisms

If there is a procedure in place for baptisms, this should continue. The churchwardens should liaise with the clergy taking the service to explain what normally happens. If there is no set system, the churchwardens will need to ensure that the clergy know what they are being asked to do.

Someone should be responsible for baptisms in church, ensuring that there is:

• water (slightly warmed!) for the font

- a candle (where this is the practice of the church)
- a completed baptism certificate
- an entry in the baptism register
- baptism service sheets or booklets.

Weddings

A different person might take responsibility for weddings. The tasks include:

- arranging an organist
- liaising with the flower arrangers
- opening up the church for a rehearsal
- ensuring that the registers are written up and the certificate completed before the service begins
- arranging to give out the service sheets or booklets and, if necessary, hymn books
- collecting the fees for the PCC and the sequestration account
- paying clergy (where appropriate), organist, choir, verger, bellringers, etc.

Funerals

The area/rural dean and churchwardens should draw up a list of clergy for undertakers to approach regarding funerals. The undertakers also need a point of contact with someone from the parish where there is to be a church service. This person will be responsible for:

- ensuring that the time chosen for a funeral is suitable from the church's point of view
- opening up the church at least 30 minutes before the service (and ensuring it is warm in the winter!)
- arranging an organist
- checking the details with the person taking the service
- arranging to give out the hymn books and service booklets
- clearing up after the service
- collecting the fees for the PCC and the sequestration account.

For a burial in the churchyard, additional tasks include:

- arranging with the undertaker for the grave to be dug
- meeting with the gravedigger to show where the body is to be buried, or clearly marking the grave site
- completing the entry in the burial register.

Where there is a churchyard, it is advisable for the churchwardens to have:

- a plan of the churchyard
- the procedure for deciding where people are buried
- details of the guidelines for headstones and other monuments.

The outgoing vicar should have passed on this information.

Keeping Records

Parish records are extremely important historical and legal documents. Enter baptism, wedding and burial registers in permanent ink. The diocesan office or local registrar can advise on the ink to use and where to obtain it. The rules are not so strict on service registers but they are still permanent documents and a fountain pen with permanent ink is more appropriate than a biro. If there is someone in the parish who has neat and tidy writing, ask that person to enter the registers. Inform that person of *all* church services and house communions in order to enter the details in the service register in advance.

Pastoral Care

Most clergy have an important ministry of pastoral care. In a growing number of parishes clergy share this ministry with lay people. In others, the vicar works this out in his or her own way. The scope of this pastoral care will vary. In some parishes there will be regular visiting of the sick and bereaved. Others will place an emphasis on visiting newcomers to the church or parish. Some will see the main work among church attenders, perhaps with an emphasis on supporting those who have key roles in the church. Others will encourage good neighbourliness rather than official church visiting.

When there is no vicar, the churchwardens and the PCC will have to arrange for appropriate pastoral care. As we suggested earlier, it is important to discover what the outgoing vicar did. This may need a degree of sensitivity. Many clergy feel that they do not do enough visiting. Any implied criticism of the vicar's approach to visiting may make it difficult for him/her to share in an open and honest way.

Some of the areas to address are:
- preparation of parents and godparents of children being baptised
- preparation of wedding couples
- visiting the bereaved
- welcoming newcomers
- visiting the sick at home
- visiting the sick in hospital
- visiting of regular church attenders
- care and support of church officers and those responsible for key areas of the church's work.

The outgoing vicar may also take communions to the sick or housebound, as well as to homes for the elderly or nursing homes. It may be necessary to reduce the frequency of these communions. Alternatively, it is possible and increasingly common for lay people, with the consent of the bishop, to take the consecrated bread and wine to the sick and homebound following the main Sunday service.

As we suggested in chapter 1, it is helpful to consider any change in practice before the vicar leaves. Many parishes involve lay people in these activities. At a diocesan level, the person responsible for lay ministry may be aware of courses to equip people in listening skills and to train them as visitors.

If, when the vicar leaves, there is little lay involvement in visiting and pastoral care, consult with the area/rural dean. Consider what support he/she can offer and the resources that may be available in the deanery.

Chapter 7

Practical arrangements

The Parsonage House

Before the vicar moves out of the parsonage house, find out the location of the

- stopcock
- gas meter
- electricity meter
- electrical fusebox
- telephones.

Find out how the following items operate (and locate the instruction booklets):

- heating system
- burglar alarm
- smoke alarm
- photocopier
- fax
- parish computer.

On the day of the vicar's departure:

- check the oil tank level (for oil-fired heating systems)
- receive the keys to the house, security locks, garage, outbuildings, church(es) and church buildings.

Many dioceses produce clear guidance on the maintenance of the parsonage house when it is unoccupied. Check the advice we offer against the advice from your diocesan office.

General maintenance

One of the churchwardens, or a person acting on their behalf, should keep a regular check on the parsonage house, visiting it at least once a week. Ensure that all the appropriate people at the diocesan office and the area/rural dean know whom to contact for access to the house. All property deteriorates when unused. Arrange to clean the gutters, service the boiler (if this is not on a service contract) and switch the water off. During the winter period, run the heating system to provide frost protection.

Repairs

In most dioceses, the Parsonage Board is responsible for undertaking repairs to the property. When the vicar moves out, contact the person in the diocesan office with responsibility for parsonage houses. Normally he/she will arrange for someone to visit the house and assess what repairs are necessary.

The Diocese promised to make some improvements at the Vicarage

Decoration

The incoming vicar is usually responsible for the internal decoration of the parsonage house. If this involves substantial work then the appropriate body at diocesan level may offer some help and the PCC asked to make a contribution.

Fuel

The outgoing vicar should also arrange for readings of the gas and electricity meters in the week before he/she moves and pay the final invoice. A churchwarden should arrange readings in the week before the new vicar moves in. The costs of minimal heating charges can be met from the sequestration account. If the parsonage house has oil-fired central heating, estimate the oil in the tank when the outgoing vicar leaves and pay the vicar for the remaining oil from the sequestration account. When the new vicar arrives he/she can pay for the oil remaining into the sequestration account.

Post

Ensure that the outgoing vicar arranges with the Post Office to redirect all mail. Tell the diocesan office where to send mail. This will normally be one of the churchwardens. Make sure that the person receiving the diocesan mail passes on relevant items to the appropriate person in the parish and keep items that the new vicar will need.

Garden

If there is someone with an interest in gardening, ask him or her to maintain the garden. Costs for basic upkeep can be met from the sequestration account.

Office equipment

It is probably best to move the photocopier, computer, fax and answer machine away from the parsonage house once it is empty.

Telephone

Arrange to have incoming phone calls diverted to another number. Arrange for a bar on outgoing calls from the telephone in the parsonage house.

Sequestration

If nothing else, churchwardens will probably learn one new word during that time when there is no vicar. That word is 'sequestrator'. In legal terms, a sequestrator takes possession of property or funds and in ecclesiastical terms this relates to the income for the benefice. The churchwardens and the area/rural dean automatically become the sequestrators under the Church of England (Miscellaneous Provisions) Measure 1992. The diocesan registrar normally advises the churchwardens and area/rural deans of their duties as sequestrators. The role of sequestrator also includes the maintenance of services, care for the parsonage and preparation for the arrival of the new vicar.

The sequestrators are responsible for the receipts and payments when there is no vicar. Each diocese operates these accounts in a different way so check on the procedure in your diocese. The Board of Finance office normally organises this. If a separate account is opened, a bank mandate is necessary. It is likely to be easier if the advice is to keep a separate column in the PCC's accounts. However, this will require close liaison with the PCC treasurer.

Pay in clergy fees for weddings and funerals to this account. Pay out clergy fees, where applicable and at the diocesan rate, and travel expenses to visiting clergy from this account. Some dioceses also pay licensed readers from it; others have a separate licensed readers' fund. It is important that you obtain details of the fee required and the car mileage expenses from each person taking a service. Pay these at the end of each month or quarter. If you decide to pay these out of church collections or to pay cash, keep accurate records of all transactions.

Pay all legitimate expenses relating to this period when there is no vicar, including expenses incurred by the sequestrators, out of this account. This includes basic heating and garden upkeep. However, it is advisable to check with the appropriate person in the diocesan office for full details of what you can and cannot pay from the sequestration account.

Chapter 8

Finding a new vicar

The Appointments Procedure

Since 1989 the appointment of a new vicar follows the procedures set down in the Patronage (Benefices) Measure 1986. When the vicar resigns, retires or dies, the bishop gives notice of the impeding vacancy to the diocese's 'designated officer' who informs the patron or patrons and the secretary of the PCC or PCCs.

PCC meetings (known as section 11 meetings)

Within four weeks of this notice, the PCC (jointly if a multi-parish benefice) must hold one or more meetings (from which the outgoing vicar, spouse and patron are excluded) to deal with six items:

1. Preparing a statement describing the conditions, needs and traditions of the parish (see 'Parish profile' below).
2. Electing two lay members of the PCC to act as the parish representatives in connection with the selection of a new vicar. Where this involves more than one PCC, each PCC has the right to elect at least one member to represent it. If the meeting fails to elect two representatives, the churchwardens take on this role (see 'Parish representatives' below).
3. Deciding whether to ask the patron to advertise the vacancy. The patron's agreement is necessary and the PCC may have to cover the costs involved.
4. Deciding whether to request a joint meeting with the patron and the bishop (see 'Section 12 meeting' below).
5. Deciding whether to request a statement in writing from the bishop

describing, in relation to the benefice, the needs of the diocese and the wider interests of the church.

6. Deciding whether to pass a resolution under section 3 (1) or (2) of the Priests (Ordination of Women) measure 1993.

Meeting of the PCC, patron and bishop (known as the section 12 meeting)

The PCC, the patron or the bishop can request a Section 12 meeting. Some bishops always call for such a meeting, others are more selective. A meeting must be convened within six weeks of any request. The area/rural dean and the lay chair of the deanery synod must be invited to attend. The PCC secretary convenes the meeting for which at least 14 days' notice is necessary. The patron and the bishop may send representatives to the meeting. At least one-third of the PCC must attend, and the outgoing vicar and his spouse are again excluded. The purpose of the meeting is to exchange views on:

- The PCC's statement describing the conditions, needs and traditions of the parish
- The bishop's statement (verbal if no written statement has been requested) describing, in relation to the benefice, the needs of the diocese and the wider church.

Suspension of presentation

The bishop may decide to seek the consent of the Diocesan Pastoral Committee to suspend presentation. This is most likely to happen where there is a possibility of pastoral reorganisation although there are other circumstances that may lead a bishop to ask for a suspension. "Presentation" describes the procedure by which a patron presents a priest to the bishop to be instituted to the freehold of the benefice. Under the Pastoral Measure 1983 the bishop has to consult the patron, PCC and the area/rural dean and lay chair of the deanery synod, giving reasons for considering suspension and taking the comments of others into account. If the living is suspended, it is important that consultation about pastoral re-organisation is addressed separately from, and prior to, the section 12 meeting.

Parish Representatives

The role of the parish representatives is to discover the will of God for the future of their parish and to share in the process of selecting a new vicar. They are elected by the PCC to act on its behalf and the people of the parish. It is their responsibility to interview the candidate suggested by the patron. The churchwardens are not necessarily the right people to be the parish representatives. Others with more experience or a wider understanding of the parish may be more appropriate.

Parish Profile

The PCC's statement describing the conditions, needs and traditions of the parish is often known as the parish profile. Some parishes will have carried out a mission or parish audit that may well cover similar ground. You do not have to wait for the vicar to go before you draw up a profile. It may be better to do it when the vicar is still in post. Some parishes complete a parish profile every five years, possibly updating it each year. It can form an essential part of the development of a mission strategy and therefore becomes a normal part of church life.

In drawing up a parish profile, remember that many organisations also have an interest in the community and may have gathered information that is of value to the parish. Begin by drawing up a list of voluntary organisations that provide services within the parish. These may include the Parish Council, hall committee housing associations, children's and youth groups, women's groups, Rural Community Council, organisations with a concern for the elderly and for those with disabilities. It is likely that there will be members of the church involved with some if not all of these groups and these people may be the first point of contact.

The national census provides information broken down into small areas on population, age range and social groupings, car ownership, travel to work, employment and housing. County, district and parish councils have this information. Some communities, particularly in rural areas, carry out village appraisals. The Parish Council usually organises such appraisals but there is nothing to stop any community organisation, including the church, initiating it. The appraisal includes a method for assessing the value put on local amenities and the infrastructure by local people as well as expressions of opinions about needs in the community. Such an appraisal may include questions about the work of the church.

There is no set way of doing a parish profile. However, it is likely to include the following:

- The community in which the church is set
- The different aspects of church life
- The use of church buildings
- Parish finances and administration.

Person Profile

In some way the PCC has to make clear the type of vicar it will prefer. Some will list expertise in every ministry whereas others will focus on one aspect only. It is better to strike a balance somewhere between the two. One way is to draw up a list of essential and desirable qualities, say five of each, as in the example below:

Qualities	Essential	Desirable
Good preacher	✔	
Visitor of the bereaved	✔	
Interested in children's work	✔	
Enthusiast for new styles of worship	✔	
Collaborative style of leadership	✔	
Encourager of others	✔	
Interested in young people	✔	
Concern for marginalised in our community		✔
A good listener		✔
Ability to teach others		✔

Having completed a person profile, it should normally be included with the parish profile for consideration at the section 12 meeting. This document provides information that the patron and bishop needs in order to find a suitable candidate to send to the parish.

Everyone has their own idea about the sort of Vicar they want

Interviewing the Prospective Vicar

The church has a unique way of making appointments. The patron chooses a candidate to whom he/she wishes to offer the benefice and informs the PCC representatives and the bishop. The bishop and both the PCC representatives have to agree before the patron makes an offer. If any of them say 'no' the patron has the option of referring the matter to the archbishop. In some situations the bishop is the patron and he informs the PCC representatives of his chosen candidate. The same system applies, with both PCC representatives having a right of veto.

Traditionally, the patron selects one candidate at a time as the most suitable person at that point to be considered for the post. If that candidate is not acceptable, in due course the patron suggests another person for interview. In other cases, two or three candidates will be invited at the same time.

The first meeting with a prospective candidate will allow for a mutual exploration, deciding whether to move on to the next stage. At this stage, there will be an opportunity for the candidate to see the vicarage and the church/churches and be taken on a conducted tour of the parish/parishes.

The parish representatives and the candidate (and his/her spouse where this applies) will raise questions in an informal atmosphere. Whether the candidate meets senior laity, including licensed readers, at this stage or at the next stage along with the formal interview, is a matter of judgement. Others who might meet the candidate at this stage include potential clergy colleagues (especially in a team or group ministry), clergy from other denominations in the area and key people in the community, such as the head teacher in a church school. Their views might be helpful in choosing the right person. In all this confidentiality is absolutely essential.

The next stage will include the formal interview. In interviewing, the parish representatives are attempting to discover how the candidate, if appointed, will fit into the life of the parish. Parish representatives should be familiar with the parish profile and the person profile produced for the section 12 meeting. They should also have read the candidate's curriculum vitae and be ready to ask questions about it. As well as checking out the qualities looked for in the new vicar, the underlying approach of the

The interview panel was restricted to just one churchwarden from each parish

candidate is important. Does his/her personal faith come through? Is there an enthusiasm for ministry? Is there sensitivity to those of different opinions?

Make arrangements in advance over procedures regarding the spouse. He/she will not normally be part of the formal interview and the parish representatives should make proper arrangements for his/her care during that time.

Choose a place for the interview that provides a relaxed atmosphere. Inform the candidate of the length of the interview. Questions should be as open as possible, drawing out the candidate to share his/her approach to ministry. Avoid questions that have a built in bias or may elicit yes/no responses.

There are a number of key areas of ministry to explore. The parish representatives' task is to discover the approach of the candidate in each area and to communicate the approach of the parish, as far as they understand it, to these issues. We suggest they include:

- Worship – perhaps exploring approaches to all age worship, music in worship, values of the Common Worship, BCP and newer liturgical material
- Preaching – purpose of preaching, the sources of sermon material
- Pastoral care – general approach, sharing visiting with lay people, attitude to those who want their child baptised, how to manage conflict
- Spiritual life – how to encourage people in their prayer life, approach to spiritual growth
- Theology and the Bible – how to keep up to date with theological issues, approach to Bible study
- Ministry and team work – understanding of ministry, involvement of lay people, example of working with other churches
- Mission and evangelism – understanding of mission, approach to evangelism
- Social issues – how the church engages with them, views on remarriage after divorce, views on homosexuality
- Children and young people – experience in work with children and young people, views on children and communion

- Education and learning – how to develop Christian learning, attitude to church and state schools
- Administration – approach to PCC meetings, administrative skills
- Personal development – approach to time off, leisure activities and interests outside the church
- Ecumenism – experience of working ecumenically and attitude towards ecumenical co-operation
- Interfaith issues – attitude to other faiths.

Making the Decision

Having met the candidate, it is the parish representatives' responsibility to decide whether he/she is the right person. Normally the patron will have carefully chosen the candidate and the bishop will most probably have approved the choice before sending him/her to the parish for interview. If the parish representatives have any doubts over the suitability of the candidate, it is open to them to share their concerns with the patron and the bishop or archdeacon.

There will be situations where, after prayer and careful consideration, the parish representatives feel that this person will not be right for the parish. They should give reasons for their decision and not rely solely on intuition. The patron or bishop may well question their decision so they need to be sure of their reasoning. In addition the patron or bishop may well tell the candidate why he/she is not being offered the post. This may well help them, through careful reflection, to see the type of parish or work to which God is calling them. Similarly, if a candidate turns down an invitation to the parish, the reasons given may well help the parish to reassess their expectations.

Announcing the Decision

Once a candidate accepts the invitation to become vicar of the parish, discussions take place on when to announce this in the vicar's present parish and the parish to which he/she is to move. This announcement is usually made in both parishes on the same Sunday.

Looking Forward to a New Vicar

Following the announcement of the name of the new vicar, there may be some people who argue that everything is left until he or she arrives. Some may begin to say things like "When the new vicar comes, we will be able to do something about . . .". If you are not careful, everything is put on hold and the new vicar becomes the sole focus of church life. In some situations, these can turn into almost "messiah-like" expectations. No new vicar can meet all these expectations. There may also be those who begin to wind down, ready to hand their job "back to vicar" as soon as possible after the service of institution. It is important to keep on doing what you have been doing during the time when there is no vicar.

Article from a parish magazine

The standard rule about chain letters is to throw them in the bin and forget about them. However this light hearted one is worth a read.

If you are unhappy with your vicar, simply ask your churchwardens to send a copy of this letter to six other churches who are tired of their vicar. Then bundle up your vicar and send him to the church at the top of the list. Within a week you will receive 16, 435 vicars, one of whom should be just right.

PS One church broke the chain and received its old vicar back!

Chapter 9

Saying hello

Welcoming the New Vicar

Settling in to a new home and area takes time. Whilst the social event that follows the institution of a new vicar to a parish is an important milestone for the parish, for the new vicar the many faces can blur and be forgotten. All is new for the vicarage family. The pressure of the pastoral and worship round often means that there is no chance to get a feel of the context of the church's work. It is important for the vicar to have space in the first few days and weeks.

The churchwardens in particular have the best opportunity of sharing the innermost culture of the parish during this period. Churchwardens who offer to brief the new vicar will help to ensure a smooth introduction to the life of the parish. The churchwardens also provide a point of reference to the new vicar as he/she begins to establish his/her ministry in the parish. An open house invitation by at least one churchwarden to the new vicar is an important gesture. This will often lead to a deep level of trust developing that can be an important marker for a growing church. Such friendships often endure.

Practical help is often welcome when moving house. However, be sensitive and offer help that the new vicar and his/her family will appreciate. This may be an opportunity to involve one or two people on the fringe of the worshipping life of the church.

Institution and Induction

The service of institution and induction varies from diocese to diocese. Several dioceses are now producing the service on computer disk, which is then personalised, for each particular institution and induction. Churchwardens need to clarify their role in the organisation of the service and the social event that normally follows the service. A meeting with the area/rural dean will help in determining who is responsible for what. Where there is more than one parish, one example of good practice is for the bishop and the new vicar to pray with the churchwardens in each church before the institution service.

The PCC will probably be involved in the arrangements for the service and the refreshments that follow it. This is an important event in the life of the church, the start of a new phase of ministry. Invitations to all members of the churches for which the new vicar will have responsibility should be given in the services leading up to the institution service.

Some people will need a specific invitation and the PCC secretary usually sends this out. The list of those invited will vary from parish to parish but will probably include:

- clergy and licensed readers of the deanery
- clergy of other denominations in the area
- clergy and licensed readers who have taken services during the vacancy
- the deanery synod lay chairman or woman and the diocesan secretary.

It is normal practice to invite spouses, with a specific invitation to the spouses of the bishop, archdeacon and area/rural dean.

Invitations to representatives of the local community might include:

- head teachers of schools in the parish/parishes
- the local member of Parliament
- the mayor or chairman of the local council
- representatives of local voluntary organisations, businesses and other institutions
- local authority youth and community advisers, local doctors and the police.

In planning for this service, remember to notify the police about one month before the service, especially if there are parking problems or other safety factors. Parking should be reserved for the bishop, archdeacon, area/rural dean, registrar and the new vicar if the vicarage is not within walking distance. Normally they will also have exclusive use of the vestry. A decision will have to be made on where clergy and licensed readers will robe. Remember to secure any room where personal items are kept.

The First Sunday

The first Sunday following the service of institution and induction is another significant stage in this new relationship. Some members of the church will have been unable to attend the service of institution and others will have had little opportunity to talk to the new vicar. If possible, allow time after each service on the first Sunday, perhaps over coffee, for the new vicar to meet as many people as possible. Where there is more than one church, this may require a slight adjustment to service times. In a benefice with more than one parish, it may also be sensible to include an act of welcome in the first service the vicar takes in each church.

Idea from *The Sign We Give*

During an act of worship, there was an exchange of gifts to welcome the new priest:

'Some of us from the parish gave him gifts to symbolise what we are as a parish, our history and strengths and needs. We gave him a sweat-shirst with school logo, because the school is very important to us, and the parish council minutes book, and a box of biscuits to show we he settles here. He gave us a South American blanket, from his work there, and a picture of Archbishop Romero for the church, and a candle, to symbolise prayer. It felt like agreeing to share our lives, priest and people together. It was a good start.'

from *The Sign We Give* – Roman Catholic Bishops of England and Wales (Arthur James Publishing).

Saying Thank You

During this time between vicars, there probably has been a number of visiting clergy and licensed readers providing worship cover. Once the new vicar is in place, they may appreciate a letter of thanks from one of the churchwardens or the PCC secretary. In this letter, acknowledge the special gifts and contributions they have brought to enrich the congregational experience of worship.

Working with the New Vicar

The churchwardens have a key role in the early stages of working with the new vicar. If they are sensitive to what has happened during the time the parish has been without a vicar, they will be in a position to offer invaluable advice to the new vicar.

An early meeting of the new vicar, churchwardens and church members involved in overseeing the key areas of church life is essential. The new vicar and the PCC will have to decide whether those who have taken on responsibility during this period should carry on. In coming to a decision, it may be necessary to examine several factors. In the first place, consider how effectively each task was performed. Where it was done well, was this due to the person or group taking responsibility for it or were there other reasons? Where it was not done well, what were the reasons? In the second place, consider whether some people carried a disproportionate load during this time without a vicar and should be relieved of some of the burden. In the third place, consider the strengths of the new vicar and decide how best to use the gifts and skills which he/she brings in organising the work of the church. There may need to be more than one meeting before making final decisions.

The 'Honeymoon Period'

The first three-six months in a new vicar's ministry is sometimes described as the 'honeymoon period'. There is often a tremendous amount of goodwill at this stage. At the same time, through the welcomes and the settling in period, the new vicar is weighing up the church and its people and they are watching how he/she handles the sensitive issues of church life. It is a time of anticipation and excitement but also uncertainty and anxiety.

The new vicar may be wrestling with conflicting feelings and emotions, at times absolutely convinced of God's call to this parish and at other times wondering whether it was the right decision. As well as observing the new vicar, some lay people are likely to approach the vicar to enlist his/her support for their particular interest. Others may wish to remain in or become part of the 'inner circle', however that is perceived.

Whilst recognising their own hopes and fears, the churchwardens can have a key role in supporting the new vicar through this early period. By offering an opportunity in confidence to share feelings and talk openly about the developing relationship between the vicar and members of the church, the churchwardens can create a close bond that will be a source of strength in this critical period.

Clergy are human too. As the churchwardens and new vicar share in the ministry, and the relationship grows, the stresses on those who minister will become apparent. The churchwardens and the new vicar need to find a way of caring for and supporting each other.

She rang the bell for each year she meant to stay

And Finally

This book needs to be read alongside the helpful advice and information available in many dioceses. We cannot emphasise too strongly how important it is to begin planning long before the vicar leaves. When you hand over to the next churchwarden encourage him/her to read this book and share any significant insights you have gained.

Resources and Further Reading

Booklets on the Interregnum

Situation Vacant: A Guide to the Appointment Process in the Church of England – David Parrott and David Field (Grove Books 1996)
A comprehensive guide through the Appointments Procedure with some suggestions on good practice for parish representatives.

Understanding the Interregnum: Making Judgements When Kings Move – Tony Bradley (Grove Books 1996)
Explores scriptural examples of gaps between God's appointed leaders and offers two programmes for parish consultancies during an interregnum.

General Books

A Handbook for Churchwardens and Parochial Church Councillors – Kenneth MacMorran and Timothy Briden (Mowbray 2001)
Often known as the churchwardens' 'bible', this book offers a guide through the church's legal and procedural matters.

Practical Church Management: a guide for every parish – James Behrens (Gracewing 1998)
A comprehensive and practical guide to the essential aspects of church life.

Some Worship Resources

The Common Worship Lectionary (Church House Publishing) *and* The Lectionary according to Common Worship and the Book of Common Prayer (SPCK).
Published each year these cover the Sunday and daily readings from Advent Sunday.

Visual Liturgy: service and worship planning software (Church House Publishing)
This comprehensive package will help in the planning of worship. It includes the official texts from Common Worship.

Patterns for Worship (Church House Publishing) – also available with Visual Liturgy
Service outlines, resources sections and suggestions on how to put together worship services.

Word Among Us (Year A), Word of Truth (Year B), Word in our Time (Year C) Commentaries on the Lectionary Readings – Martin Kitchen, Georgiana Heskins and Stephen Motyer (Canterbury Press 1998–2000)
These volumes cover the readings for Years A–C in the Revised Common Lectionary.

Living Stones: Complete Resource Books for Years A, B & C – Susan Sayers (Kevin Mayhew 1997–1999)
Notes on the Common Worship readings, discussion starters, background material for an all age talk, programmes for children and young people, intercessions and music suggestions for every Sunday.

Clouds of Glory: Prayers for the Church's Year (Year A) – David Adam (SPCK 1998) *and* Traces of Glory: Prayers for the Church's Year (Year B) – David Adam (SPCK 1999) *and* Glimpses of Glory: Prayers for the Church's Year (Year C) – David Adam (SPCK 2000)
Three books of prayers (one for each year of the Common Worship lectionary) that link to the readings for each Sunday.

Seasons and Celebrations: Prayers for Christian Worship Book 1 – Donald Hilton (National Christian Education Council 1996) *and* The Word in the World: Prayers for Christian Worship Book 2 – Donald Hilton (National Christian Education Council 1996)
Book 1 has prayers for each season of the Christian year and for special Sundays; Book 2 has prayers on a variety of themes.

All Desires Known – Janet Morley (SPCK 1992) *and* Bread for Tomorrow: Praying with the World's Poor (SPCK 1992)
Devotional and inspirational prayers designed for worship in a variety of settings.

Leading Intercessions – Prayers for Sundays and Holy Days, Years A, B & C Raymond Chapman (Canterbury Press 1997 and 2000) *Scripture-related intercessions following the customary five-fold pattern of prayer for the church, the world, the community, the sick and the departed.*

Cloth for the Cradle: Worship Resources for Advent, Christmas and Epiphany (Wild Goose Publications) *and* Stages on the Way: Worship Resources for Lent, Holy Week and Easter (Wild Goose Publications)
Includes litanies, meditations, monologues, poems, prayers, readings, scripts and symbolic actions.

Sing God's Glory: Hymns for Sundays and Holy Days, Years A, B & C – compiled by Alan Luff and others (Canterbury Press 2001)
Provides a comprehensive guide to choosing Scripture-related hymns and worship songs for each Sunday and major festival.

Your diocesan resource centre or Christian bookshop will probably have many of these and similar resources.